PUFFIN BOOKS

The Father Christmas It's a Blooming Terrible Joke Book

Ϋ ̄ ̄ ̄ways gets the sack every time he goes to work?
Ϝ ̄ ̄ Christmas!

I ̄ ̄ ̄ Christmas loves jokes! He has a large collection,
v ̄ ̄ ̄ enjoys telling to Dog and Cat, and especially to the
reir ̄ ̄ vhen he is travelling round the world delivering
pr ̄ ̄ or taking his holidays. Here is a sackful of Father
C ̄ ̄ 's favourite jokes as an extra special present for
yo ̄ ̄ joy. Open it up! Inside you'll find reindeer jokes,
y ̄ ̄ ales, snow jokes, and many others. You don't have
to ̄ til Christmas – have lots of blooming fun now!

RAYMOND BRIGGS

Presents

The Father Christmas

Compiled by Karen King

Illustrated by Rowan Clifford

PUFFIN BOOKS

PUFFIN BOOKS

Published by the Penguin Group
Penguin Books Ltd, 80 Strand, London WC2R 0RL, England
Penguin Putnam Inc., 375 Hudson Street, New York, New York 10014, USA
Penguin Books Australia Ltd, 250 Camberwell Road, Camberwell, Victoria 3124, Australia
Penguin Books Canada Ltd, 10 Alcorn Avenue, Toronto, Ontario, Canada M4V 3B2
Penguin Books India (P) Ltd, 11 Community Centre, Panchsheel Park, New Delhi – 110 017, India
Penguin Books (NZ) Ltd, Cnr Rosedale and Airborne Roads, Albany, Auckland, New Zealand
Penguin Books (South Africa) (Pty) Ltd, 24 Sturdee Avenue, Rosebank 2196, South Africa

Penguin Books Ltd, Registered Offices: 80 Strand, London WC2R 0RL, England

www.penguin.com

First published in Puffin Books 1994
19

Text copyright © Raymond Briggs/Blooming Productions Ltd, 1994
Illustrations copyright © Raymond Briggs, 1994
All rights reserved

The moral right of the author/illustrator has been asserted

Made and printed in England by Clays Ltd, St Ives plc

British Library Cataloguing in Publication Data
A CIP catalogue record for this book is available from the British Library

ISBN 0–140–37354–3

www.greenpenguin.co.uk

Contents

Christmas Crackers

Christmas. The busiest time of the year for me. It's work, work, work from the beginning of November right up to blooming Christmas Day. First I have to sort out the Christmas lists everyone has sent me, then get the presents ready, wrap them all up and load them on the sledge. And Cat and Dog are under my feet all the time, getting in the blooming way. One year I even wrapped up Cat by mistake! Didn't realise until I was all ready to set off, then heard her miaowing. I couldn't work out where she was at first but Dog soon sniffed her out. Trouble is, he knocked all the presents off the sledge because Cat was right at the bottom! I had to load them all back up again – after I'd unwrapped Cat, of course.

Then the reindeer and I have to deliver the presents all over the blooming World. Not an easy task, I can tell you. Travelling in the cold, dark night through snow, rain, hail and fog. So what I do to cheer myself up is to tell myself jokes. Then I thought, there's a lot of people who need cheering up too so why not share my favourite jokes with them?

Happy blooming reading!

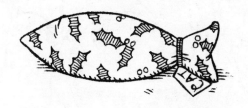

Knock! Knock!
Who's there?
Mary!
Mary who?
Mary Christmas.

Where do ghosts go at Christmas?
To a phantomime.

What do monkeys say at Christmas?
Jungle bells, jungle bells.

Why are Christmas trees like bad knitters?
They both drop their needles.

What's Christmas called in England?
Yule Britannia.

What did the skeleton say when he received a comb for Christmas?
Thanks – I'll never part with it.

Why is a burning candle like a thirst?
Because a drop of water puts an end to both of them.

Girl: I had a wonder watch for Christmas. Every time I look at it I wonder if it's still going.

Gary: What did you have for Christmas?
Steve: A mouth organ. It's the best present I've ever had.
Gary: Why?
Steve: My mum gives me £1 a week not to blow it.

What do you get when you cross an apple with a
Christmas tree?
A pine-apple.

Knock! Knock!
Who's there?
Miss.
Miss who?
Miss-l-toe is nice at Christmas.

Did you know that workers in a candle factory are
paid by the wick?

Lady: What did you give your little brother for
Christmas?
Girl: Measles!

What do you give a train driver for Christmas?
Platform shoes.

What do elephants sing at Christmas?
Noel-ephants, Noel-ephants . . .

Burglar: The police arrested me for doing my
Christmas shopping early.
Lawyer: They can't do that.
Burglar: It seems they can. They caught me in the
shop at three in the morning.

What do sheep sing at Christmas?
Ewele-tide Carols!

Jack: Do you like the dictionary I bought you for
Christmas?
Jill: Yes, I do. I just can't find the words to thank
you enough.

Jimmy: Mum, do you know what I'm going to buy you for Christmas?

Mum: No, dear. What?

Jimmy: A nice teapot.

Mum: But I've already got a nice teapot.

Jimmy: You haven't now. I've just dropped it!

Mary: Which burns longer, a white candle or a red candle?
Sam: Neither. Candles burn shorter, not longer.

Nick: You've just written a cheque for £100.
Steve: I know – it's a Christmas present for my sister.
Nick: You forgot to sign it.
Steve: No, I didn't. I'm sending it anonymously.

As shepherds washed their socks by night,
All seated round the tub,
A bar of Sunlight soap came down,
And they began to scrub.

What did the big candle say to the little candle?
I'm going out tonight.

What do misers do in cold weather?
Sit round a candle.

What do misers do in very cold weather?
Light it!

As shepherds watched their flocks by night,
All tuned to BBC,
The angel of the Lord came down,
And switched to ITV.

Knock, knock!
Who's there?
Wenceslas.
Wenceslas who?
Wenceslas bus – I want to get home!

What happens to you at Christmas?
Yule be happy.

How can you tell the time with a candle?
Listen to the candles-tick.

Boy: My Dad bought me a watch for Christmas
that's shock-proof, waterproof, anti-magnetic and
unbreakable.
Friend: What's the time, then?
Boy: I don't know – I've lost it.

A woman went to the pet shop to buy a parrot for
her little girl for Christmas.
   'I want a parrot for my little girl,' she told the
man.
   'Sorry,' said the man. 'We don't do swops.'

Mum: Are you going to Susie's Christmas party,
John: No, I ain't.
Mum: What have I told you about saying 'ain't'? I
am not going, he is not going, she is not going, they
are not going.
John: Blimey, ain't no one going?

Sally had written out all her Christmas cards and
was busy sticking stamps on the envelopes ready to
post them.
   'You've put too much postage on that card, Sally,'
Mum told her.
   'Oh dear, I hope it doesn't go too far then,' Sally
said worriedly.

Paul: How long does a candle take to burn down?
Jane: About one wick.

Why did Jimmy's aunt knit him three socks for Christmas?
Because his mother wrote and told her he had grown another foot.

What did the Christmas cracker say to a friend?
My pop's bigger than your pop!

What did one candle say to the other?
You're getting on my wick.

Harry's aunt was staying with them for Christmas.

'Here are two apples,' she said to Harry, handing him a large apple and a small one. 'Share them with your sister.'

So Harry gave the small apple to his sister and kept the large one for himself.

'You are mean,' said his sister. 'If aunt had given me the apples, I'd have given you the large one and kept the small one for myself.'

'Well, that's the one you've got,' said Harry, 'so what are you moaning about?'

What do you call someone who gets a tool box for Christmas?
Andy.

After eating a big Christmas dinner Peter went straight out to play. Half an hour later he came in groaning and holding his tummy.

'What's the matter?' asked his mother. 'Are you in pain?'

'No,' said Peter. 'The pain's in me.'

BOOKS FOR CHRISTMAS

Unusual Pets by Terry Dactyl
Do It Yourself by Andy Gadgett
Rice Growing by Paddy Field
Keep Fit for All by Horace Zontalbars
Swimming the Channel by Francis Near
Simple Mathematics by Algy Brar
Home Heating by Arthur Mometer
Springtime by Teresa Greene.
Hark to the Singing! by Harold Angels
The First Noel by Carol Singer

Father: What would you like for Christmas, Sam?
Sam: I've got my eye on a new bike.
Father: Well, keep your eye on it, son. Because
you'll never get your bottom on it.

Did you hear about the little girl who wanted to buy
her Grandma some hankies for Christmas but
couldn't remember the size of her nose?

What happens if you eat Christmas decorations?
You get tinselitis.

What made the baby candle feel warm all over?
Glowing pains.

PRESENTS YOU CAN'T BUY

A button for a coat of paint.
A saddle for a clothes horse.
Sheets for an oyster bed.
Music for a rubber band.
False teeth for a river's mouth
Shoes for a walking stick.

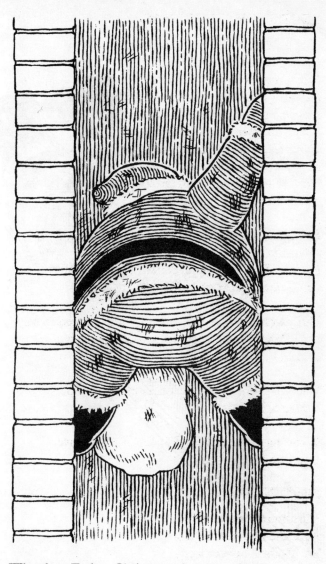

Why does Father Christmas always go down
chimneys?
Because it soots (suits) him.

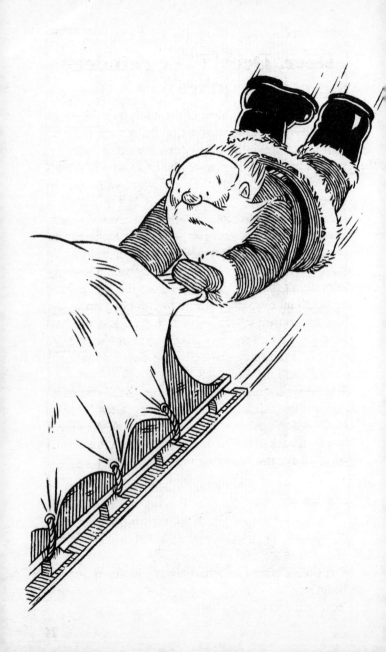

Deer, Deer! (The reindeer jokes)

I love reindeer jokes. Most of them anyway. There's a couple in this section that I don't think are quite so blooming funny, but the deer insisted I included them. They said they were their favourites. You'll soon know which ones they are when you come to them.

Reindeer quite like jokes about themselves as long as they're *funny jokes*, and not jokes that make fun of *them*, if you see what I mean. They can get really huffy about it. No sense of humour. Once I told a joke my deers didn't like and they tore across the sky, jerking the sleigh all over the place. I had to cling on to the sides to stop myself falling off. I even lost my hat. Good job I'd tied the presents on tight or they'd have gone too. I felt quite queasy by the time I'd managed to calm them down.

Anyway, me and the deers put our heads together and came up with this selection of jokes. There's one or two they don't like but I expect they think they'll get their own back in the Father Christmas section. Huh! Not if I have my blooming way, they won't!

What do reindeer say before they tell you a joke?
This one will sleigh you.

Why is a reindeer like a gossipy person?
Because it's a tail (tale) bearer.

Why do reindeer wear fur coats?
Because they'd look silly in plastic macs.

How do you make a slow reindeer fast?
Don't feed it.

How long should a reindeer's legs be?
Long enough to reach the ground.

Why did the reindeer wear black boots?
His brown ones were at the menders.

Why did the reindeer wear sunglasses on the beach?
He didn't want to be recognised.

Which reindeer have the shortest legs?
The smallest ones.

Where do you find reindeer?
It depends where you leave them.

Did you hear about the reindeer who bought a
sleeping bag?
He spent two months trying to wake it up.

Boy: I can lift a reindeer with one hand.
Other boy: Huh! I bet you can't.
Boy: OK. Show me a reindeer with one hand and
I'll lift it for you.

How many legs does a reindeer have?
Six: fore-legs in front and two at the back.

What's the difference between a biscuit and a reindeer?
You can't dunk a reindeer in your tea.

What's brown, has two antlers and counts to ten backwards?
A reindeer with hiccups.

Two reindeer were talking. One asked the other, 'How was the stag party?'

What happened to the reindeer who swallowed an Oxo cube?
He made a laughing stock of himself.

What is the reindeers' favourite game?
Stable tennis.

What do reindeer have that no other animals have?
Baby reindeer.

When should you feed reindeer milk to a baby?
When it's a baby reindeer.

Why did the reindeer take a ruler to bed with him?
So he could see how long he slept.

What kind of umbrellas do reindeer use in heavy rain?
Wet ones.

First polar bear: Look! That reindeer's ready to help pull Father Christmas's sleigh.
Second polar bear: How can you tell?
First polar bear: He's got no-el plates.

What do you call a reindeer in a desert?
Lost.

First reindeer: Where do fleas go in winter?
Second reindeer: Search me.

When is a child not a child?
When it is a little deer.

How do you make a reindeer stew?
Make it wait for a few hours.

Why did the reindeer chase its tail?
It was trying to make ends meet.

What did Mrs Christmas say to her husband during the storm?
'Come and look at the reindeer!'

What did the cobbler say when a herd of reindeer walked into his shop?
Shoo!

If a reindeer lost his tail, where would it go for a new one?
To a retail shop.

What did Father Christmas do when the reindeer chewed his favourite book?
Took the words right out of his mouth.

Why don't reindeer like penguins?
They can't get the wrappers off.

Why do reindeer scratch themselves?
Because they're the only ones who know where they itch.

Why did the reindeer laze in the sun?
Because he wanted to tan his hide.

What did the dog say to the reindeer?
Woof! Woof!

How do you know when there's a reindeer in your bed?
It's got an R on its pyjamas.

What's the difference between a sick reindeer and a dead bee?
One's a seedy beast and the other's a bee deceased.

How is a reindeer like a grape?
They're both purple except for the reindeer.

How do you get a reindeer into a matchbox?
Take out the matches first.

What's big, brown and delicious?
A chocolate-covered reindeer.

What did the hungry reindeer say when he only had thistles to eat?
Thistle have to do.

What has two heads, one tail, four eyes, two antlers and a long white beard?
Father Christmas on a reindeer.

There was a young reindeer from Surrey,
Who cooked up a large pot of curry,
   He ate the whole lot,
   Straight from the pot,
And ran to the tap in a hurry.

What is the wettest animal?
A reindeer.

Did you hear about the reindeer who stayed up all
night to try to work out what happened to the sun
when it went down?
It finally dawned on him.

There was a young reindeer from Kent,
Whose nose was all battered and bent,
  One day he arose,
  And followed his nose,
And no one knew which way he went.

There was a reindeer from Quebec,
Who once wrapped his legs round his neck,
  But then he forgot,
  How to undo the knot,
And now he's an absolute wreck.

What do you call a large one-eyed deer who lends a helping hand?
Good idea.

What do you call a deer with no eyes?
No idea.

What do you call a deer with no eyes, nose, ears or legs?
Still no idea.

Why did the reindeer jump up and down?
He'd forgotten to shake his medicine.

How does a reindeer get up a tree?
He sits on an acorn and waits for it to grow.

How does a reindeer get down a tree?
He sits on a leaf and waits for autumn.

Do you know the story of the three deer?
Dear, dear, dear.

When is a nail like a reindeer?
When it's driven.

How do you make a reindeer fly?
Buy it an airline ticket.

There once was a reindeer called Dewy,
Who wouldn't eat meat that was chewy,
  Nor the milk, nor the fish,
  That was put on his dish,
He'd only eat piles of chop suey.

Teacher: Tell me an animal that lives in Lapland.
Boy: A reindeer, Sir.
Teacher: Good! Now tell me one more.
Boy: Another reindeer.

What do you get if you cross a reindeer with a worm?
Big holes in the garden.

How is a reindeer on a fence like a ten pence piece?
Its head is on one side and its tail on the other.

What do you do with a green reindeer?
Wait until it ripens.

What do you do with a blue reindeer?
Try to cheer it up.

Travellers' Tales

I go all over the world on Christmas Eve, but I'm too busy to see much of it. And it's too blooming dark, anyway! So in the summer I make my sledge into a camper-van and I go off on my holidays. I've been everywhere . . . France, the good old U.S.A. and even far-flung places like Scotland. Had a marvellous time, too. Mind you, I have to keep moving on when people recognize me. Doesn't do for Father Christmas to be spotted sun-bathing in Las Vegas, does it? Upsets folk a bit. They think I should be stuck at the North Pole all year round. Can't think why. Even the blooming Queen has a holiday!

Anyway, I've learned a thing or two on my travels, I can tell you. And one of the things I've discovered is that people all over the world love a good joke. So I've collected a few here that are sure to make you chuckle. Cheer you up no end, they will. *Au revoir, mes amis.* That's another thing I learned, a bit of French. Pretty impressive, eh? *Très bon!*

What do people in Scotland eat?
Tart-an-pie.

Which town in Britain makes terrible sandwiches?
Oldham.

What did the tourist write on the postcard from Cuba?
Havana good time.

Boy: I'm glad I don't live in France.
Friend: Why?
Boy: I can't speak French.

What's the coldest country in the world?
Chile.

Why do French people eat snails?
They don't like fast food.

Where do you find exploding pasta?
At the minestrone of Defence.

Teacher: Who can tell me where the Andes are?
Boy: On the end of my armies.

What do you call a very small man who works on
the Paris underground railway?
A metro gnome.

How do you greet a German barber?
Good morning, Herr Dresser.

There was an old farmer in Spain,
Who prayed very hard for some rain,
  The resultant showers,
  Lasted for hours,
And washed his farm right down the drain.

What Spanish dance do people do at the end of summer?
The tan-go.

Who was the famous Italian artist who used to sit on ice cubes?
Bottichilli.

What does a German eat in a Chinese restaurant?
Sweet and sour-kraut.

Did you hear about the Italian who went to Scotland
for a holiday?
He got lost in the mist and became known as the
'Roman in the gloamin''

There was a young lady of Rheims,
Who had the most terrible dreams.
   She would wake in the night,
   In a terrible fright,
Shaking the house with her screams.

What famous London detective loved bubble baths?
Sherlock Foams.

Did you hear the one about the Scotsman who
washed his kilt and then couldn't do a fling with it?

Did you hear about the man who jumped into the
river in Paris?
The police said he was in-Seine.

What's French and very relaxing?
A long loaf.

A cowboy saw a dog disappear over a cliff one day.
What did he say?
'Doggone!'

What's a good way to make your money go a long
way?
Fill your wallet with notes, then fly to Timbuctoo.

Why is a Greek island like the letter T?
Because it's in the middle of water.

Where's Hadrian's wall?
Round Hadrian's house.

There were two flies in the airing cupboard. Which
one was Scottish?
The one on the pipes.

Knock! Knock!
Who's there?
Juan.
Juan who?
Juan of us might as well open the door.

There was a young lady from Ryde,
Who ate some green apples and died,
    The apples fermented,
    Inside the lamented,
And made cider inside her inside.

What happens when you throw a green stone in the
Red Sea?
It gets wet.

What's the laziest mountain in the World?
Mount Ever-rest.

What airline do fleas travel on?
British Hairways.

What kind of biscuit do you find at the South Pole?
A penguin.

What is the Cheddar Gorge?
A very large cheese sandwich.

What do you get if you cross an American president with a shark?
Jaws Washington.

Did you hear about the two peanuts touring New York?
One was a-salted.

How did the Paris police find Quasimodo?
They followed a hunch.

If a man was born in England, lived in America all his life, and died on holiday in Spain, where would he be buried?
In the ground.

Where do sheep go for their holidays?
The Baa-haa-maas.

What do you get if you dial 666?
The Australian police.

How do ghosts travel abroad?
By British Scareways.

What's very tall and wobbles over the streets of Paris?
The Trifle Tower.

What do you do if the M6 is closed?
Drive up the M3 twice.

What is the widest rope in the world?
Europe.

What's mad and goes to the moon?
A loony module.

When do spare parts for Japanese cars fall out of the sky?
When it's raining Datsun cogs.

What did the Spanish farmer say to his chickens?
Olé!

What's big and hairy and flies to America?
King Kongcord.

Why is the Pacific like an idea?
Because it's just a notion.

How do Welsh people eat cheese?
Caerphilly.

Did you hear about the Spanish lady who had identical twins?
She couldn't tell Juan from the other.

A charming young singer called Hanna,
Got caught in a flood in Savannah,
  As she floated away,
  Her sister, they say,
Accompanied her on the pianna.

What language do twins speak in Holland?
Double Dutch.

If Ireland fell into the sea which part would float?
Cork.

Who are the two largest women in America?
Mrs Sippy and Miss Oury.

Dad, I don't want to go to Australia!
Shut up and keep digging!

Why was the Egyptian girl worried?
Because her daddy was a mummy.

A man and his wife had just arrived at the airport after a long and tiring journey.

'I wish I'd brought the piano with me,' the husband said wearily.

'What on earth for?' demanded his wife.

'I left the plane tickets on it,' he sighed.

How did the toad cross the Channel?
By hopper-craft.

Where do the Chinese make motor car hooters?
Hong King.

What made Wales gradually sink into the sea?
All the leeks.

What animal with two humps is found at the North Pole?
A lost camel.

What do you call a Russian who robs lemonade factories?
Knock your pop off.

If all the cars in Britain were pink what would you have?
A pink-car nation.

Why is a guide book like a pair of hand-cuffs?
Because it's for tourists (two-wrists).

What language do they speak in Cuba?
Cubic.

Did you hear about the African cat that escaped from the zoo?
He made the headlions.

What's grey and sits in a tree singing 'Hoots mon, hoots mon?'
A Scottish owl.

First railway porter: I had a terrific struggle getting a woman's trunk onto the Crewe train.
Second porter: Why, was it heavy?
First porter: No. She wanted to go to Portsmouth.

Woman: I say, guard, where is this train going?
Guard: This train goes to Liverpool in ten minutes, madam.
Woman: Good gracious! Last time I went to Liverpool it took four hours.

Why is a stupid boy like the Amazon jungle?
They're both a little dense.

48

Harry was telling his friend about his holiday in Switzerland. His friend had never been to Switzerland and asked, 'What did you think of the scenery?'

'Oh, I couldn't see much,' Harry told him. 'There were all those mountains in the way.'

Why is honey scarce in Brighton?
Because there's only one B in Brighton.

Two cowboys got lost in the desert of Arizona. They were starving, when one of them shouted: 'Look! Food at last! There's a pork-pie tree . . .'
He galloped off, but a few minutes later he came back, with arrows sticking out of his hat. 'Shucks,' he said. 'That wasn't a pork-pie tree. It was an am-bush.'

A country policeman cycling down a lane was astonished to see a hiker walking bent under the weight of a large signpost which read TO PLYMOUTH.

''Allo, 'allo, 'allo!' said the policeman, getting off his bike. 'What are you up to with that, then?'

'I'm walking to Plymouth, constable,' explained the hiker, 'and I don't want to lose my way.'

MARVELLOUS JOKE, THIS! MY FAVOURITE!

Teacher: What are the chief minerals to be found in Cornwall?
Pupil: Coca Cola and orangeade, Sir.

There was an old man from Penzance,
Who always wore sheet-iron pants,
   He said, 'Some years back,
   I sat on a tack,
And I'll never again take a chance!'

There once was a lady from China,
Who sailed off on an ocean liner,
   She slipped on the deck,
   And twisted her neck,
Now she sees what's happening behind her.

What made the Tower of Pisa lean?
A strict diet.

The dachshund's a dog of German descent,
Whose tail never knew where his front end went.

Where do Arabian cats come from?
The Purrsian Gulf.

It's Snow Joke!

Blooming snow. I hate it! Makes me shiver just thinking about it. Cat and Dog don't care for it much either but the reindeer don't seem to mind it. Mind you, with their thick fur coats they don't feel the cold like I do. Chills me right down to my old bones, it does. No matter how close I sit by the fire I can't seem to get warm.

I know you children think snow is marvellous. You like to build snowmen, have snowball fights, go sledging and other such stuff. Can't think why; you must be freezing to death. Wait till you get to my age! You won't cheer when you wake up and see snow on the ground then, I can tell you.

If I had my way there'd be no snow jokes in this book, but they all wanted some. Write some jokes about snowmen and suchlike, they said, the children like them. So this section of jokes is especially for you. But don't expect me to laugh at them. As far as I'm concerned there's nothing funny about snow at all. *Brr!* Blooming horrible stuff!

What happened when the snowgirl fell out with her boyfriend?
She gave him the cold shoulder.

What do snowmen wear on their heads?
Ice caps.

What's an ig?
An Eskimo's home without a loo.

Knock! Knock!
Who's there?
Snow.
Snow who?
Snow good asking me!

What do snowmen eat for lunch?
Iceburgers.

Where do snowmen go to dance?
To snowballs.

How does a snowman travel around?
By icicle.

What sort of ball doesn't bounce?
A snowball.

What do you get if you cross a snowball with a shark?
Frost bite.

What do you call an Eskimo's cow?
An Eskimoo.

How do you know there's a snowman in your bed?
You wake up wet.

What is white, furry and smells of peppermint?
A polo bear.

What's the difference between an iceberg and a clothes brush?
One crushes boats and the other brushes coats.

Why did the snow-drop?
Because it heard the cro-cus.

Which two letters of the alphabet do snowmen prefer?
I.C.

Where do snowmen keep their money?
In a snowbank.

What did the snowman order at McDonalds?
Icebergers with chilli sauce.

What stays hot even at the North Pole?
Mustard.

How did the snowman make anti-freeze?
He put ice-cubes in her bed.

Knock! Knock!
Who's there?
Igloo.
Igloo who?
Igloo knew Susie like I know Susie.

Snowgirl: Where's your mum come from?
Snowboy: Alaska.
Snowgirl: Don't bother, I'll ask her myself.

What do you call a penguin in the Sahara desert?
Lost.

What's ice?
Skid stuff.

Snowman: Is it true that you can jump off a high
snowy mountain without hurting yourself?
Other snowman: No, that's just a bluff.

Snowman: (outside the igloo): Was it you who had
the house-warming party last night?

Boy: Can I share your sledge?
Friend: Sure, we'll go halves.
Boy: Gosh, thanks!
Friend: I'll have it to go downhill and you can have
it to go uphill.

A lady watched as a boy and his sister stood by a frozen pond. The boy handed his ice skates to his sister.

'Here, you can have first go,' he said.

The lady went over to the boy. 'That was very kind of you to let your sister skate first,' she said.

'I wanted to see if the ice was thick enough,' the boy told her.

Knock! Knock!
Who's there?
Snow.
Snow who?
Snow use, I've lost the little card with my name on it!

How did the snowman keep himself cool at the football match?
He sat by the fans.

What's it called when two snowmen fight?
An icebox.

What meat do snowmen like to eat?
Cold cuts.

Mary: What did you think of the film we saw about the Abominable Snowman?
Jack: It left me completely cold.

Knock! Knock!
Who's there?
Gutter.
Gutter who?
Gutter get in, it's snowing out here!

Why did the Abominable Snowman toss three people at a time into the icy water?
Because his mother told him: 'Two's company, freeze a crowd.'

Snowman: Did you hear about the cricket match between two teams of snowmen in which no one was out?
Polar bear: Yes – that was the match when they kept bowling sNOw balls.

What's a snowman's favourite song?
There's no business like snow business.

Do you know how polar bears see each other in all
that snow?
They've got very good ice sight.

What did the Eskimo wife say to her husband when
he had finished building the igloo?
What an ice little house.

Have you heard about the eskimo who found a way
to keep the roof on his house?
Iglood it.

Knock! Knock!
Who's there?
Willis.
Willis who?
Willis snow never end?

Boy: Do you think it will snow today?
Friend: That all depends on the weather.

Two mountaineers got into difficulties and one found himself hanging on a rope over a snowy precipice. While his friend was vainly trying to heave him to safety, the rope began to fray.

At this the one hanging on the rope shouted, 'What happens if the rope breaks?'

'Don't worry,' said his pal. 'I've got another one!'

There was a young fellow called Fisher,
Who was fishing for fish in a fissure,
  When a seal, with a grin,
  Pulled the fisherman in;
Now they're fishing the fissure for Fisher.

Baby penguin: Are you sure I'm a penguin?
Mother penguin: Why do you ask?
Baby penguin: Because I'm freezing!

Knock! Knock!
Who's there?
Ann.
Ann who?
Ann Tartic.

Knock! Knock!
Who's there?
Eskimo.
Eskimo who?
Eskimo questions, I'll tell you no lies.

What's white and goes up?
A silly snowflake.

What fish do you need if you're on ice?
Skate.

Two men got stuck in a snowdrift, but only one got
his hair wet. Why?
The other one was bald.

What ship would you take to a party?
An ice-breaker.

When is a boat like a heap of snow?
When it comes a-drift.

Lovely grub!

I always say that the best part of Christmas is the grub!
Lots of lovely things to eat, turkey, mince pies, ham,
Christmas pud, plenty of tomato ketchup. Crumbs,
my mouth's watering just thinking of it!

Funny thing is, I know lots of jokes about food but
I couldn't think of one about tomato ketchup. Not one
single one. The reindeers and I wracked our brains but
we just couldn't come up with a single ketchup joke.
Can't understand it! Ketchup's so fan-blooming-tastic
I could almost eat it by itself. Maybe that's why there's
no jokes about it. It's too marvellous to joke about.

Anyway, you'll find lots of good jokes about grub in
this section. I've saved the very best jokes till last. The
'waiter, waiter' jokes. Blooming marvellous they are.
My favourite. Made me laugh so much my sides
ached! Mind you, it's not so funny when you're in a
restaurant and you actually find a blooming fly in your
soup or whatever. And these things do happen, believe
me. You wouldn't believe the things I've been served
when I've been on my hols around the world. It's
enough to put you off your grub!

Noah: I thought we had two turkeys when we started out.
Mrs Noah: Well, dear, it is Christmas.

Why is the turkey a fashionable bird?
Because he always appears well-dressed for dinner.

If a waiter was carrying a turkey on a platter and he dropped it, what three great disasters would occur?
The downfall of Turkey, the breaking up of China and the overthrow of Greece.

Why is a guitar like a turkey being made ready for the oven?
Because they are both plucked.

There once was a fat boy called Kidd,
Who ate twenty mince pies for a quid.
   When asked, 'Are you faint?'
   He replied, 'No, I ain't.
But I don't feel as well as I did.'

How do you make an apple puff?
Chase it round the garden.

What do you call a man with jelly in one ear and
sponge cake and custard in the other?
A trifle deaf.

How do you start a jelly race?
Get set.

What stands on one leg and has its heart in its head?
A cabbage.

What's the best thing to put into a mince pie?
Your teeth.

What's bread?
Raw toast.

Knock! Knock!
Who's there?
Felix.
Felix who?
Felix my ice cream I'll lick him!

Knock! Knock!
Who's there?
Lettuce.
Lettuce who?
Let us in and you'll find out.

What's yellow and stupid?
Thick custard.

When's a turkey like a ghost?
When it's a goblin.

What's brown and sneaks around the kitchen?
Mince spies.

Shall I tell you the joke about the butter?
No, I'd better not, you'll only spread it.

What's bad-tempered and goes with custard?
Apple grumble.

What cake gives you an electric shock?
A currant bun.

What flies and wobbles?
A jellycopter.

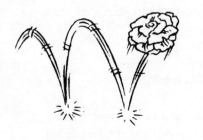

What's green and goes boing-boing-boing?
Spring cabbage.

What's the best day for frying sausages?
Fry-day.

How do you make a sausage roll?
Push it.

Why are cooks bullies?
They whip the cream and beat the eggs.

Where do good turkeys go when they die?
To oven.

What vegetable goes best with jacket potatoes?
Button mushrooms.

Which tree is full of food?
The pantry.

Did you hear the joke about the orange?
It was juicy.

What nuts can you hang pictures on?
Walnuts.

What's the rudest food?
Sausages – because they spit.

Did you hear about the fight in the biscuit tin?
The penguin got hit by a club and the bandit got away in a taxi.

Knock! Knock!
Who's there?
Goose.
Goose who?
Goose who's knocking on your door?

Why did the girl keep a mince pie in her comic?
She liked crummy jokes.

Girl: Mum, this chicken has dots on it.
Mum: It's OK, it's only chicken pox.

Why was the soup rich?
Because it had 14 carrots in it.

Did I tell you the joke about the empty jar?
There's nothing in it.

What's the fastest vegetable?
A runner bean.

Knock! Knock!
Who's there?
Irish Stew.
Irish stew who?
Irish stew in the name of the law!

What do you get if you cross an egg white with gunpowder?
Boom-meringue.

Why is a leg of pork like an old radio?
You get crackling from both.

What did the two salt-cellars say after they'd had a fight?
Shake.

What did the egg say in the monastery?
Oh well, out of the frying pan into the friar.

There was once a boy called Freddie,
Who ate several helpings of jelly,
  Then rhubarb and custard,
  And sausage and mustard,
Which gave him a pain in the belly.

BLOOMING SILLY! HE SHOULD HAVE STARTED WITH THE SAUSAGE!

What's red and goes *Beep! Beep!*
A strawberry in a traffic jam.

What do you call five bottles of lemonade?
A pop group.

Why did the egg go into the jungle?
He was an eggsplorer.

Where should the twenty-pound banana go?
On a diet.

Why did the jelly wobble?
Because it saw the milk shake.

Why is a banana-skin like a pullover?
Because it's easy to slip on.

What swings from cake to cake?
Tarzipan.

What do you give a sick lemon?
Lemonade.

Why should you never tell secrets in a
greengrocer's?
Because potatoes have eyes and beanstalk.

What's purple and hums?
An electric plum.

A venturesome three-week-old chamois
Strayed off in the woods from his mammois,
    And might have been dead,
    But some picnickers fed
Him with sandwiches, milk and salamois.

Dog's Favourite Book:
COOKING FOR DOGS by Nora Bone.

What parts of a river can be eaten?
The source (sauce) and the current (currant).

What do you get when you cross a dog with a chicken?
Pooched eggs.

What dog has no tail?
A hot dog.

What is the definition of a doughnut?
A crazy millionaire.

What's round, white and giggles?
A tickled onion.

What did the baby chicken say when its mother laid an orange?
Look what mama laid.

The cat is the one animal that never cries over spilt milk.

Where did Noah keep his bees?
In the archives (ark hives).

What do you call two rows of cabbages?
A dual cabbageway.

A tramp knocked on the door of a house to beg for something to eat.
'Do you mind eating yesterday's soup?' asked the lady.
'Not at all,' said the tramp.
'Good,' said the lady. 'In that case, come back tomorrow.'

Waiter, waiter, this coffee tastes like mud.
I'm not surprised, madam. It was only ground a moment or so ago.

Waiter, waiter, this lobster's only got one claw!
It's been in a fight, sir.
Well, bring me the winner!

Waiter, waiter, you've got your thumb on my steak.
I know, sir. I don't want it to fall on the floor again!

Waiter, waiter, this egg tastes off.
Don't blame me, sir. I only laid the table.

Waiter, waiter, I'd like some fish.
Come this way sir, and I'll find you a plaice.

Waiter, waiter, this soup tastes funny!
So why don't you laugh?

Last-minute Addition!

Got a letter this morning from Fred. Would you believe it – there were two ketchup jokes in it! Just in time, too, for me to put in this bit. I'm going to try them out on Dog.

What did the hamburger say to the tomato?
That's enough of your sauce.

Guess what happened when the tap, the dog and the tomato took part in a race?
The tap was running, the dog took the lead, and the tomato tried to ketchup.

Feline Funnies and Canine Capers

My best audience for jokes are Cat and Dog. Whatever I'm doing at home – wrapping presents, digging the garden, making a pot of tea – they're around. So I tell them a lot of jokes. I always know if they think a joke is extra funny, because Cat purrs and Dog makes a whuffley barking noise. If I'm sitting in my armchair in the evening, Cat gets on my shoulders and rubs her head against mine, and Dog puts his head on my lap.

Over the years, they've heard a good many jokes, and they like different kinds. But Cat's favourites are about dogs – silly dogs, not friendly clever ones like Dog. She also likes jokes about mice, fish, birds and so on. Dog likes jokes about cats (not Cat – the other kind)! Here are some of the jokes they like best of all.

What did the dog say when the train ran over his tail?
'It won't be long now.'

Why did the cat run away when you shouted at her?
You hurt her felines.

What do a dog and a tree have in common?
Bark.

Jim: I've lost my dog.
Jack: Well, why don't you put an ad in the paper?
Jim: Don't be daft – he can't read.

What do you get if you cross a ball of wool with a cat?
Mittens.

Teacher: The essay you wrote on the topic MY DOG is exactly the same as your brother's.
Pupil: Yes, I know. It's the same dog.

What did the cat say when the dog caught him by the tail?
'That's the end of me.'

What's a puppy's favourite cartoon character?
Pupeye the Sailor.

What is a puppy's life like?
Ruff.

What happened to the puppy who got laryngitis?
He felt totally yelpless.

What do you call a dog with a bunch of daisies on its head?
A collie-flower.

I LIKE CAULIFLOWERS-COOKED WITH CHEESE SAUCE!

Someone complained to Father Christmas that Dog had been chasing a man on a bicycle.

'Don't be silly,' said Father Christmas. 'Dog can't ride a bicycle.'

What is an eight-sided cat?
An octopus.

What do you call a fish with no eyes?
Fsh.

What do they call kittens in the Wild West?
Posse cats.

What happened when the cat swallowed some coins?
At last there was some money in the kitty.

What do you call a thin mouse?
A narrow squeak.

When is a dog like a camera?
When it snaps.

When is a black dog not a black dog?
When it's a greyhound.

Why did the cat eat cheese?
So he could blow down the mousehole with baited
breath.

What's the best place for a cat to go on holiday?
The Canary Islands.

LOST DOG:
Black and white, three legs, right ear missing, blind
in one eye, eight teeth missing, bushy tail, answers
to the name Lucky.

Why was the dog called Johann Sebastian?
Because of his Bach.

What do you do if you wake up in the middle of the
night and hear a mouse squeak?
Oil it.

Where do dogs keep their money?
Barklay's Bank.

A man was about to go on the escalator in a shop
when he saw a notice: 'Dogs must be carried on this
escalator'. By the time he had found a dog, the shop
was closed.

What's the difference between a tiny elephant and a
gigantic mouse?
About 2,000 pounds!

How do you stop a dog digging holes in your
garden?
Hide his spade.

Why did Cat join the Red Cross?
He wanted to be a first aid kit.

There was a man who thought he was a dog. He ate dog food for supper, slept curled up at the foot of the bed, and barked when he heard noises in the night. His doctor treated him for six months, and at the end of that time the man seemed to have recovered. He ate sitting on a chair at the table, watched television and talked to people without barking. His doctor said it was time to end his treatment, and the man was very pleased.

'I know I'm better now,' he said. 'Just feel how cool my nose is.'

Two cats met in an alley.
'Meow' said the first.
'Bow-wow' the second answered.
'What kind of a reply is that?' the first cat asked, arching its back.
'I'm learning a foreign language,' the second cat replied proudly.

Which dog is the most expensive of all?
A deer hound.

Joe: How do you spell mouse trap using only three letters?
Jane: CAT.

Cat: There were two mice in the airing cupboard. Which one was in the army?
Dog: I don't know. Which one was in the army?
Cat: The one near the tank.

What goes tick woof, tick woof, tick woof?
A watch dog.

What type of dog goes into a corner every time a bell rings?
A boxer.

What kind of dog hides from frying pans?
A sausage dog.

There were twenty cats in a boat out at sea. One jumped out. How many were left?
None – they were all copy-cats.

Why do cats change their size?
Because they are let out at night and taken in in the morning.

What do you get if you cross a cat with a chemist's?
Puss in Boots.

John: Why is your cat so small?
Jill: He was brought up on condensed milk.

Did you hear about the sheepdog that had her puppies in a rubbish bin?
It said PLACE LITTER HERE on the front.

What is Cat's favourite breakfast?
Mice crispies.

What wears a coat all winter and pants all summer?
A dog.

What do you call a cat that eats lemons?
Sourpuss.

Newsflash: Forty pedigree dogs stolen from kennels.
Police say they have no leads.

There was a young lady named Maggie,
Whose dog was enormous and shaggy;
  The front end of him
  Looked vicious and grim –
But the tail end was friendly and waggy.

Why did the boy call his pet dog 'Blacksmith'?
Because every time someone called, the dog made a
bolt for the door.

How do you stop a dog from barking in the back seat of a car?
Put him in the front.

Why did the dog howl?
Because he was barking up the wrong tree.

Where do you take a sick dog?
To the dogtor.

Teacher to Mary: Define 'dog show' for me.
Mary: Oodles of poodles.

Doctor: Don't you know that my hours are only from 2–4 pm?
Patient: Yes, I do. But the dog that bit me doesn't.

Dog: Did you hear about the dog who likes to have a bath four times a day?
Cat: No. What kind of a dog is it?
Dog: A shampoodle.

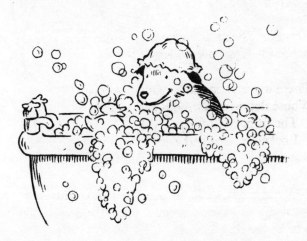

Father Christmas

Guess who? I've actually found some jokes about ME! Marvellous, isn't it? I could hardly believe it at first. Then I thought, why not? What would Christmas be like without me? Who else would be daft enough to work their fingers to the bone delivering all those blooming presents? That's why I'm called Father Christmas, isn't it?

Some of these jokes are a bit cheeky! In fact, if I knew who made them up there'd be no Christmas presents for them this year, I can tell you. I suspect the deer have something to do with it, trying to get their own back for the reindeer jokes. Anyway, it just goes to show how famous I am if there are jokes all about me. Makes me feel really important, I can tell you. But I don't want to brag too much so I've kept this section short. And I've saved it to last so you can finish the book with a really good chuckle!

Happy Blooming Christmas, everyone!

What do you get if you cross Father Christmas with a detective?
Santa Clues.

Father Christmas won a saucepan in a competition. That's what you call pot luck.

Father Christmas: Every year, I deliver presents to the two children of a florist. One's a budding genius, the other's a blooming idiot.

What do the reindeer sing to Father Christmas on his birthday?
Freeze a jolly good fellow.

What do you call a man who claps at Christmas?
Santapplause.

Twinkle, twinkle, chocolate bar,
Santa drives a rusty car,
    Press the starter,
    Press the choke,
Off he goes in a cloud of smoke.

Who delivers presents to baby sharks at Christmas?
Santa Jaws.

Why does Father Christmas like to work in the garden?
Because he likes to hoe, hoe, hoe.

Snow, snow, go away,
Come back on another day,
When I'm not riding in my sleigh.

Not long ago Santa developed a fear of closed-in places and refused to go down any more chimneys. His illness was diagnosed as Santa-Claus-trophobia.

Why is a cat on the sea-shore like Christmas?
Because both have sandy claws (Santa Claus)

What does Father Christmas call his money?
Iced lolly.

When Father Christmas stops delivering presents
for a few minutes to have a rest, it's known as a
Santa pause.

Father Christmas was asked how he liked his work.
He replied, 'It has its ups and downs.'